STUCK IN PLACE

Navigating the Challenges of an Unsold Home

Morgan C Sloan

KDP

Copyright © 2024 Morgan C Sloan

All rights reserved

The characters and events portrayed in this book are fictitious. Any similarity to real persons, living or dead, is coincidental and not intended by the author.

No part of this book may be reproduced, stored in a retrieval system, or transmitted in any form or by any means, electronic, mechanical, photocopying, recording, or otherwise, without express written permission of the publisher.

ISBN-13: 9798333346483
ISBN-10: 1477123456

Cover design by: Art Painter
Library of Congress Control Number: 2018675309
Printed in the United States of America

LEGAL DISCLAIMER

The information provided in this book, "Stuck in Place: Navigating the Challenges of an Unsold Home," is for general informational and educational purposes only. The author and publisher of this book have made every effort to ensure that the information provided herein is accurate and true, but they make no claims, promises, or guarantees about the accuracy, completeness, or adequacy of the contents of this book and expressly disclaim liability for errors and omissions in the content.

This book does not offer legal, financial, or any other professional advice. If professional assistance is required, the services of a competent professional should be sought. The scenarios and advice outlined in this book are not intended to serve as a substitute for personalized advice from a qualified professional.

All information in this book is provided "as is," with no guarantee of completeness, accuracy, timeliness, or the results obtained from the use of this information, and without warranty of any kind, express or implied, including, but not limited to warranties of performance, merchantability, and fitness for a particular purpose.

The publisher and the author shall not be liable to you or anyone else for any decision made or action taken in reliance on the information provided in this book or for any consequential, special, or similar damages, even if advised of the possibility of such damages.

The laws and regulations governing real estate transactions vary widely from location to location and are subject to change. The examples and strategies discussed in this book are based on general circumstances and may not apply directly to individual cases or in different geographic areas.

Readers are encouraged to consult with professional real estate agents, financial advisors, and legal counsel to obtain advice tailored to their specific situations.

"Success is not final, failure is not fatal: It is the courage to continue that counts."

WINSTON CHURCHILL

CONTENTS

Title Page
Copyright
Epigraph
Preface
Introduction
Chapter 1: Understanding Why Homes Don't Sell   1
Chapter 2: Preparing Your Home for Sale   11
Chapter 3: Innovative Marketing Strategies   16
Chapter 4: Negotiation Tactics   25
Chapter 5: Legal and Financial Considerations   34
Chapter 6: When to Consider Alternatives   43
Chapter 7: Emotional Aspects of Selling Your Home   52
Conclusion   61
Appendices   65
About The Author   69

PREFACE

Overview Of The Housing Market

Welcome to "Stuck in Place: Navigating the Challenges of an Unsold Home," a guide designed to help homeowners navigate the complex and often frustrating journey of selling a home that won't seem to move off the market. Whether you're dealing with your first home sale or have been through this process, this book aims to provide you with a comprehensive toolkit to tackle the hurdles that keep your property from closing.

In recent years, the housing market has undergone significant fluctuations. From skyrocketing demand and soaring prices in many regions to sudden market cooling, the landscape for selling a home has become increasingly unpredictable. Factors such as economic uncertainty, changes in mortgage rates, and evolving buyer preferences have all shaped current market conditions. For instance, while low interest rates in the past few years encouraged many buyers to enter the market, recent increases have caused some potential buyers to hesitate, impacting the ease with which homes are sold.

Moreover, the rise of remote work has shifted the desirability of locations, with more buyers looking for homes in suburban and rural areas rather than city centers. This transition has left many sellers in less sought-after locations finding it difficult to attract buyers. Additionally, the surge in technology and online real estate platforms has transformed how homes are marketed and sold, emphasizing the importance of digital presence and the need for strategic online marketing.

This book is rooted in the current realities of the housing market. Each chapter is dedicated to unpacking a specific aspect of the home-selling process—from understanding why homes don't sell, to preparing your home for the market, to navigating negotiations and legal considerations. Personal anecdotes of individuals who have been in your shoes will offer real-life insights and lessons learned.

Our goal is to equip you with the knowledge and strategies to not only cope with the challenges of an unsold home but to overcome them. With the right approach, you can enhance your home's appeal, connect with the right buyers, and move forward both physically and emotionally. Let's embark on this journey together, turning stagnation into action and frustration into success.

Personal Anecdotes

Sarah's Story: Overpriced Out of the Market Sarah put her spacious four-bedroom house on the market in what she thought was a seller's market. Expecting quick offers, she priced her home above comparable listings in her neighborhood in Orlando. Weeks turned into months with very few showings and no serious offers. Discouraged and puzzled, she eventually learned through feedback that potential buyers felt her home was overpriced compared to others with similar or better amenities. Sarah's story is a classic example of the pitfalls of misjudging the market's temperature and the importance of setting a realistic price from the start.

Mike and Linda's Renovation Regret: Eager to attract buyers, Mike and Linda invested thousands into renovating their quaint Tampa Bay bungalow, updating the kitchen and the master bath, and overhauling the backyard. However, their high-end upgrades didn't resonate with the local market, where buyers were more interested in lower-cost, functional homes. The couple found themselves deep in debt from renovations that did not pay off in terms of increasing their home's sale price. Their experience underscores the critical need to understand buyer preferences in your specific market before undertaking costly renovations.

Jenna's Invisible Home: Jenna, a single mother looking to relocate for a new job, struggled to generate interest in her Orlando-area home. Despite being in a well-liked neighborhood, her home garnered little attention. It was only after hiring a new real estate agent that Jenna discovered her online listings were lackluster, with poorly taken photos and minimal descriptions. With professional photos and a more engaging listing description, interest in her home spiked, leading to a successful sale. Jenna's frustration illustrates the crucial role of digital marketing in selling a home today.

These stories reflect the various challenges homeowners face in the real estate market. Each narrative highlights specific missteps and the corrective actions that led to eventual success. As we move forward in this book, keep these stories in mind—they are real-world examples of common obstacles you may encounter and the strategic pivots that can lead to the resolution of selling your home.

INTRODUCTION

As we dive into "Stuck in Place: Navigating the Challenges of an Unsold Home," it's essential to establish what this book aims to achieve and how it can serve as a vital resource for homeowners facing the frustration of an unsold property. The goal of this book is threefold:

1. Practical Advice and Effective Strategies: First and foremost, this book is designed to arm you with actionable advice and tested strategies to enhance the marketability of your home. From understanding the importance of correct pricing to learning the ins and outs of effective marketing, each chapter is crafted to guide you through specific, realistic steps you can take to attract buyers. Whether choosing the right renovations, staging your home for showings, or leveraging the latest digital marketing techniques, you will find comprehensive guidance tailored to today's real estate market.

2. Navigational Tools for Complex Scenarios: Selling a home often involves navigating complex scenarios that can be both confusing and overwhelming. This book addresses these complexities head-on, offering insights into the legal and financial considerations that come with selling a property. From decoding contracts to planning financially while your home is on the market, the guidance provided here will clear up confusion and help you make informed decisions.

3. Emotional Support and Encouragement: Beyond the practical and logistical aspects of selling a home, "Stuck in Place"

acknowledges the emotional toll of having an unsold property on the market. This book offers emotional support and motivational advice to help you maintain your well-being throughout this challenging process. Stories from real homeowners who have been in your shoes, offering solidarity and real-world proof that your current challenges can be overcome.

By the end of this book, you should have a clearer understanding of why your home may not be selling and what you can do about it. You should also feel supported and empowered to take those steps. "Stuck in Place" is your companion in transforming a stagnant situation into a proactive, positive move forward.

CHAPTER 1: UNDERSTANDING WHY HOMES DON'T SELL

Overpricing: Common Pitfalls and How to Price a Home

One of the most frequent and detrimental mistakes homeowners make when selling their property is overpricing. Setting the right price for your home is a delicate balance that requires careful consideration of various factors. This section delves into the common pitfalls associated with overpricing and offers guidance on setting a realistic and market-friendly price.

The Psychology of Pricing: Many homeowners feel a deep personal attachment to their property and often overestimate its value, leading to an unrealistic price tag. Emotional value, however, does not translate to market value. Overpricing can stem from a range of misconceptions.

Emotional Attachment: Owners might believe their home's unique history and personalization add significant value.

Market Misunderstanding: Homeowners might only know what

constitutes a reasonable price if they have a clear understanding of the current real estate market trends and conditions.

Inaccurate Comparisons: Comparing your home to the highest-priced sale in the neighborhood without considering differences in size, condition, or location can lead to an inflated price.

The Impact of Overpricing: Overpricing a home can have several negative consequences.

Slow Market Response: Homes priced above market value tend to stay on the market longer. This delays the sale and can lead to a stigma surrounding the property. Potential buyers might wonder if there are underlying problems with a house that has been listed for an extended period.

Limited Buyer Pool: Setting the price too high from the start limits the number of potential buyers considering the property. It restricts visibility among those searching within a specific price range that matches their budget and your home's value.

Eventually Selling Below Market Value: Often, homes that start high may need to undergo several price reductions. These reductions can lead to selling at a lower price than if the house had been appropriately priced initially.

Strategies For Realistic Pricing

To avoid the pitfalls of overpricing, consider the following strategies:

Comprehensive Market Analysis (CMA): A CMA conducted by a real estate professional provides a detailed analysis of similar homes sold in your area, considering factors like location, size, features, and condition. This analysis helps set a competitive price that reflects the current market.

Professional Appraisal: Getting your home appraised by a certified appraiser can give you a good benchmark for setting a realistic price based on an unbiased assessment of your property's value.

Consider Feedback from Showings: If your home has been on the market and isn't selling, feedback from potential buyers and agents during showings can provide insight into whether the price is too high.

Stay Updated on Market Trends: Real estate markets can change quickly. Regularly updating your understanding of local market trends can help you adjust your pricing strategy as needed.

Addressing these aspects can help you avoid the common pitfalls of overpricing. Setting a realistic and strategic price for your home enhances its appeal to potential buyers and increases your chances of a quicker, more profitable sale. Remember, the goal is to align your home's listing price with its actual market value to facilitate a smooth and successful transaction.

Condition of the Property: Impact of Home Condition and Aesthetics on Buyer Interest

The condition of your property is one of the most critical factors influencing buyer interest and the eventual sale. A well-maintained and aesthetically pleasing home attracts more potential buyers and can command a higher price. Here, we explore how the physical state of your home impacts buyer decisions and what you can do to enhance its appeal.

First Impressions Matter: The initial appearance of a home can significantly affect a buyer's perception. A well-kept exterior, tidy landscaping, and a clean interior set a positive tone for showings.

Curb Appeal: This is the attractiveness of a home when viewed from the street. Enhancing curb appeal can be as simple as painting the front door, planting flowers, or ensuring the lawn is mowed and edged.

Entryway Impressions: The entryway or foyer gives potential buyers a taste of what to expect. A clutter-free, welcoming space can make a strong impression.

Key Areas of Focus: Certain areas of the home are more important to buyers and can disproportionately affect their interest:

Kitchens and Bathrooms: These rooms are crucial in the homebuying decision. Modern, updated kitchens and clean, well-functioning bathrooms are top priorities for buyers. Even minor upgrades, like new fixtures or fresh paint, can significantly enhance these spaces.

General Maintenance: Issues such as leaky faucets, cracked tiles, or peeling paint can give the impression that the home has been neglected. Addressing these issues before putting the home on the market can prevent potential buyers from being put off.

Staging the Interior: Staging involves arranging furniture and decor to showcase a home's best features. It helps buyers visualize themselves living in the space. Staged homes often sell faster and for higher prices than those not staged.

The Impact of Neglect Neglecting property maintenance can lead to a longer time on the market and potentially lower sale prices. Here's how:

Perceived Value: Buyers often estimate the cost of repairs and subtract this from the asking price, which may lead them to submit lower offers.

Inspection Issues: Problems uncovered during a home inspection may lead to delayed negotiations, reduced offers, or the buyer abandoning the deal altogether.

Enhancing Your Home's Condition To make your home more appealing, consider the following steps:

Conduct a Pre-Sale Home Inspection: Identifying and fixing problems before active marketing can avoid complications during the sale process.

Invest in Key Upgrades: If your budget allows, invest in updates that will increase the home's value and appeal, particularly in the kitchen and bathrooms.

Deep Cleaning: A deep clean can improve a home's appeal. Consider professional cleaning services, especially for carpets and windows.

Neutralize the Decor: While your home's decor is personal, overly bold or specific styles can be off-putting to buyers. Opt for neutral colors and remove personal items to help buyers envision themselves in the space.

Improving the condition of your home before listing can significantly enhance its marketability. By focusing on aesthetics and maintenance, you can create a welcoming environment that resonates with buyers, ultimately leading to a quicker sale and a better offer.

Market Dynamics: How Local and National Market Conditions Affect Home Sales

The real estate market is influenced by a complex interplay of local and national factors that can significantly impact the sale of your home. Understanding these dynamics is crucial for setting realistic expectations and making informed decisions about when and how to sell your property.

National Economic Indicators: Economic conditions at the national level can have a profound effect on real estate markets:

Interest Rates: The cost of borrowing money to buy a home is directly tied to interest rates. Lower rates generally increase buyer demand as borrowing is more affordable, whereas higher rates may deter buyers, slowing down the market.

Economic Growth: Economic indicators such as GDP growth, employment rates, and consumer confidence influence homebuying activity. A strong economy boosts buyer confidence and purchasing power, while a recession may lead to decreased demand.

Government Policies: Tax incentives, subsidies for homebuyers, or changes in housing regulations can also significantly influence market dynamics.

Local Market Trends: While national trends set the overall tone, local factors often have a more immediate and noticeable impact on home sales.

Supply and Demand: The basic economic principle of supply and demand is a critical driver in real estate markets. In areas where housing inventory is low but buyer demand is high, homes may sell quickly and at higher prices. Conversely, surplus available properties can lead to longer sale times and reduced prices.

Local Economy: The health of the local economy, including job availability, wage levels, and economic stability, directly affects the real estate market. Regions with solid job growth tend to attract more residents and, thus, more potential homebuyers.

Neighborhood Characteristics: Factors such as school quality, crime rates, and local amenities like parks, shopping, and public transportation can significantly influence the desirability of a neighborhood and, by extension, its properties.

Market Sentiment: Potential buyers' sentiments and perceptions about recent sales trends, news, or seasonal changes can also affect the local real estate market.

Adapting to Market Conditions: Given the impact of these variables, understanding how to adapt your selling strategy to current market conditions is essential:

Timing: Sometimes, the best strategy may be to wait for a more favorable market. Seasonal trends can also influence buyer activity; for example, markets are often more active in the spring and summer.

Pricing Strategy: It is critical to align your pricing strategy with the current state of the local market. This might mean adjusting expectations during a buyer's market or leveraging a seller's market to secure a better price.

Marketing Approach: Tailoring your marketing strategy to highlight what is most appealing about your property and neighborhood in light of current market trends can make your home more attractive to potential buyers.

Understanding both the broader economic context and the specific local conditions can help sellers navigate the complexities of the real estate market more effectively. By staying informed and flexible, you can maximize your chances of a successful and timely sale, even in fluctuating markets.

Poor Marketing: The Importance of Effective Marketing Strategies and Common Marketing Mistakes

Effective marketing is crucial in selling a home. It's not just about listing a property; it's about presenting it in a way that resonates with potential buyers and maximizing its exposure to the right audience. This section explores why strategic marketing is essential and highlights common mistakes to avoid.

The Role of Marketing in Home Sales Marketing a home effectively involves more than just posting an ad online. It encompasses a range of activities designed to showcase the property's best features and attract potential buyers. This includes:

Professional Photography: High-quality photos are critical as they provide the first impression of your home to potential buyers.

Compelling Descriptions: Well-crafted property descriptions should highlight unique features and selling points, appealing directly to buyers' needs and emotions.

Virtual Tours and Videos: In today's digital age, offering a virtual tour can significantly increase interest, as it allows potential buyers to experience the property remotely.

Targeted Advertising: Utilizing online platforms to target demographics likely to be interested in your property ensures that your marketing efforts reach the right audience.

Common Marketing Mistakes Many homeowners and even some agents make critical errors in marketing a property, leading to prolonged sale times and reduced interest from potential buyers. These include:

Poor Quality Visuals: Using low-quality, unprofessional photos or no photos at all can severely dampen interest in a property. The same goes for poorly executed virtual tours or videos.

Inadequate Description: Vague or uninspiring property descriptions must capture potential buyers' interest or imagination. Overlooking the importance of selling the lifestyle associated with the property is a common shortfall.

Neglecting SEO: In the digital age, search engine optimization (SEO) is crucial for making sure listings are found by buyers searching online. Ignoring SEO practices can mean your listing goes unnoticed.

Failing to Utilize All Available Channels: Relying solely on traditional methods or a single platform for marketing can limit the visibility of your listing. Effective marketing strategies use a combination of channels, including social media, real estate websites, and even local community boards.

Strategies for Effective Marketing: To avoid these pitfalls and effectively market your home, consider implementing the following strategies:

Hire Professionals: Invest in a professional photographer and consider hiring a marketing expert or a real estate professional known for their innovative marketing techniques.

Craft Engaging Content: Ensure your listing description is

engaging, highlights the unique benefits of your property, and tells a compelling story about the lifestyle it offers.

Leverage Social Media: Use social media platforms to extend the reach of your listing. This can include paid advertisements targeted at specific groups likely to be interested in your property.

Monitor and Adjust: Keep track of how your marketing strategies are performing and be prepared to make adjustments. This can involve changing your visuals, updating your property description, or adjusting your targeted advertising strategies.

Effective marketing increases your property's visibility and enhances its perceived value and appeal, making it more likely to attract potential buyers quickly. By understanding and applying these principles, you can avoid the common pitfalls of poor marketing and improve your chances of selling your home promptly and efficiently.

CHAPTER 2: PREPARING YOUR HOME FOR SALE

Home Staging Tips: Practical Advice on Staging a Home to Attract Buyers

Staging your home effectively can be a game changer in the real estate market. It's about more than just making a house look beautiful; it's about creating an environment where potential buyers can envision themselves living and thriving. Here are practical tips on staging your home strategically to maximize appeal and encourage a faster sale at a better price.

1. Declutter and Depersonalize: Start by removing personal items and clutter from your home. This includes family photos, personal collections, and any excessively bold or specific decor that might not appeal to the general public. The goal is to create a neutral backdrop that allows buyers to imagine their own lives and belongings in the space.

2. Optimize the Layout: Assess your furniture layout and room arrangements. The layout should feel open and fluid, not cramped or maze-like. Moving furniture around or even removing pieces can enhance the sense of space. Aim for a balance between coziness and spaciousness, ensuring each room has a clear

purpose and ample area to move around.

3. Update and Repair: Ensure everything in your home works well. Fix leaky faucets, squeaky doors, or loose handles. Consider making minor updates like replacing outdated hardware on cabinets, installing new light fixtures, or applying a fresh coat of paint in modern, neutral colors. These small changes can make a significant impact without a hefty investment.

4. Focus on Lighting: Good lighting is crucial. It makes spaces appear larger, more welcoming, and cleaner. Open curtains to let in natural light, and place lamps strategically in darker corners or areas to brighten them up. Ensure that all fixtures have working bulbs and consider upgrading to higher-wattage bulbs to enhance the light in the home.

5. Accentuate Key Features: Every home has unique features that can be highlighted to enhance appeal. Whether it's a fireplace, high ceilings, or large windows with a view, make sure these features stand out. This could mean arranging the furniture to showcase a beautiful bay window or adding decor that draws attention to the fireplace.

6. Neutralize the Palette: While you may love bright and bold colors, they might not be everyone's taste. Painting walls in neutral tones like beige, gray, or off-white can make your home more appealing to a broader audience. These colors also help to make rooms look bigger and brighter.

7. Add Simple Home Decor: Once you've depersonalized and neutralized your space, add some simple, stylish decor items to enhance the appeal. This could include vases of fresh flowers, a bowl of fruit on the kitchen counter, or plush towels in the bathroom. These touches add warmth and life to the home.

8. Clean Thoroughly: Before showing your home, ensure it is

immaculately clean. This includes windows, floors, surfaces, and even areas like baseboards and corners where dust and grime accumulate. Consider a professional cleaning service for a deep clean, especially in high-traffic areas like kitchens and bathrooms.

9. Create an Inviting Atmosphere: Finally, consider your home's sensory experience. A pleasant-smelling home can subtly influence buyers' perceptions. Use diffusers with mild, natural scents or bake cookies before showings to create a welcoming aroma. Ensure the home is at a comfortable temperature during showings to make potential buyers feel at ease.

Following these home staging tips, you can transform your property into an appealing and inviting space that stands out in the real estate market. Well-staged homes sell faster and often at higher prices, making the effort well worth the investment.

Essential Repairs and Improvements: Identifying and Prioritizing Repairs That Increase Home Value

Before listing your home, addressing necessary repairs and making thoughtful improvements can significantly enhance its appeal and market value. This section provides a framework for identifying which repairs are essential and how to prioritize them to maximize your return on investment.

1. Conduct a Thorough Assessment: Start by conducting a thorough walkthrough of your property to identify areas that need repair or improvement. It might be helpful to enlist a professional home inspector or contractor who can spot issues you might overlook. Focus on both cosmetic updates and deeper structural repairs. Make a list of everything from squeaky doors and peeling paint to potential plumbing or roofing issues.

2. Prioritize Based on Impact: Once you have a list, prioritize these repairs based on their potential impact on the sale. Address structural and functional issues first, as these are critical for the home's livability and can be deal-breakers if not resolved. This includes:

Roof Repairs - Ensuring the roof is in good condition is crucial, as leaks or missing tiles can lead to more significant, more costly issues.

Plumbing and Electrical Systems - Buyers value updated and fully functional systems, as problems in these areas can lead to significant expenses.

Heating and Cooling Systems - Ensure the HVAC system is efficient and in good working order, as this is a crucial selling point.

3. Focus on High-Return Improvements: After addressing any structural issues, focus on improvements that are known to offer a good return on investment:

Kitchen and Bathroom Updates - You don't need a complete remodel, but modernizing a few elements, such as faucets, cabinetry hardware, or countertops, can significantly enhance these spaces.

Painting - A fresh coat of paint in neutral colors can transform a space, making it look cleaner and larger.
Flooring: Repair or replace damaged flooring. If the carpet is old and worn, consider replacing it with a more durable and appealing option like hardwood or laminate.

4. Improve Curb Appeal: First impressions are vital, so remember the exterior of your home. Simple improvements like landscaping,

a new mailbox, a freshly painted front door, or exterior lights can significantly improve curb appeal.

5. Consider Energy Efficiency: Upgrades that improve energy efficiency can also be attractive to home buyers, especially in markets where energy costs are a concern. Consider double-pane windows, enhanced insulation, or LED lighting fixtures.

6. Don't Over-Improve: It's vital to keep your improvements in line with your neighborhood standards. Over-improving—such as installing a high-end kitchen in a moderately priced neighborhood—might not return the investment when you sell. Research similar homes in your area to see what improvements they have made before making significant investments.

7. Use Professional Help Wisely: For major repairs, use professional services. Quality workmanship in repairs and renovations can be a selling point, whereas poorly done DIY repairs can turn off potential buyers.

8. Document Improvements: Keep receipts, warranties, and a detailed list of the work done, as these can be very reassuring to potential buyers.

By carefully selecting and prioritizing repairs and improvements, you can increase your home's appeal to potential buyers, leading to a quicker sale and potentially higher selling price. Remember, the goal is to make your home stand out in the market for all the right reasons.

CHAPTER 3: INNOVATIVE MARKETING STRATEGIES

Digital Marketing: Utilizing Social Media and Online Real Estate Platforms

In the digital era, the ability to effectively market a home extends far beyond traditional methods like signage and newspaper ads. Today, digital marketing, primarily through social media and online real estate platforms, is crucial in reaching a broader audience and attracting potential buyers. This section explores leveraging digital tools to enhance your home's visibility and appeal.

1. Understand Your Platforms: Different platforms cater to different audiences and serve various purposes in real estate marketing:
   Real Estate Websites: Zillow, Realtor.com, and Trulia are specifically designed for real estate listings. These platforms are essential because they aggregate listings and draw millions of viewers actively looking to buy homes.

Social Media Platforms: Facebook, Instagram, Twitter, and Pinterest each offer unique advantages for home marketing. Instagram and Pinterest are highly visual and ideal for sharing striking images and virtual tours of your home. Facebook allows for longer posts and targeted advertising, while Twitter can be used for quick, timely updates and links to more detailed listings.

2. High-Quality Visual Content Visuals are the heart of online real estate marketing. Invest in professional photography and consider adding virtual tours or video walkthroughs of your home. These resources can be shared widely across both social media and real estate platforms:

Photos: Post high-resolution images that highlight your home's best features. Make sure each photo is well-lit, clear, and aesthetically pleasing.

Videos and Virtual Tours: These allow potential buyers to get a sense of the home's flow before visiting, making them more likely to be interested in a physical showing.

3. Engaging Descriptions: Craft compelling and detailed descriptions for your listings. Focus on your home's unique selling points and include all relevant information about the property's features, amenities, and nearby attractions or schools. Optimize your text for SEO by using keywords that potential buyers might use to search for homes.

4. Targeted Advertising Social media platforms offer powerful tools for targeted advertising, allowing you to reach specific demographics. For instance, you can target ads based on location, age, interests, and even behaviors, ensuring that your property is seen by individuals most likely to be interested in buying a home like yours.

5. Regular Updates and Interaction: Keep your listings and social media posts updated with the latest information, and interact regularly with your audience. Respond promptly to queries and comments. This keeps your listing active and builds engagement and trust with potential buyers.

6. Leverage Analytics: Use the analytics tools provided by most social media and real estate platforms to track the performance of your posts and ads. Analyze what types of content generate the most interest and engagement and adjust your strategy accordingly to maximize effectiveness.

7. Collaborate with Influencers Consider collaborating with real estate influencers or local bloggers who can help promote your property. This can increase visibility and add credibility to your listing.

By implementing these digital marketing strategies, you can significantly enhance the visibility and appeal of your home to a broad audience of potential buyers. Digital marketing broadens your reach and provides dynamic ways to present your home, making it more attractive to tech-savvy buyers who will likely start their home search online.

Open Houses and Private Showings: How to Organize Effective Open Houses and Private Tours

Open houses and private showings are crucial components of the home-selling process. They offer potential buyers a firsthand look at the property. When done correctly, they can significantly increase the likelihood of a sale by making a memorable impression. This section provides strategies for organizing effective open houses and private tours that captivate buyers and help seal the deal.

1. Timing and Scheduling: Choose the timing of your open house carefully:

Weekends: Sunday afternoons are traditionally the best time for open houses as most people are off work and available to attend.

Avoid Conflicts: Check the calendar for local events or holidays affecting turnout. Ideally, choose a day when potential buyers are not likely to be distracted by other activities.

Private Showings: Offer flexible scheduling for private tours to accommodate interested buyers who cannot make the open house or prefer a more personal viewing experience.

2. Preparation and Staging: Make sure the house is in pristine condition:

Clean and Declutter: Thoroughly clean every part of the house and remove any personal items or clutter that might distract buyers or make spaces feel smaller.

Staging: Consider hiring a professional stager to make the home more appealing. This can involve rearranging furniture, adding decor, and making the house feel welcoming and lived-in.

Repair and Renovate: Address any noticeable maintenance issues before the showing. A well-maintained home creates a better impression and reduces concerns about potential hidden problems.

3. Marketing the Event Effectively market your open house or private showing:

Online Listings: Update your online listings to highlight the open house date. Use all available platforms, including real estate websites and social media.

Signage: Place signs in the neighborhood a few days before the event to catch the eyes of passersby and local traffic.

Invitations: Send out digital invitations or flyers to local real estate agents and potential buyers who have shown interest in similar properties.

4. Providing Information: Have detailed information readily available for visitors:

Property Sheets: Provide printed sheets that include high-quality photos and critical details about the home, such as its price, dimensions, amenities, and any recent upgrades or improvements.

Neighborhood Info: Include information about the local area, such as schools, parks, transit, and nearby services, which can be important selling points for buyers.

5. Engage with Visitors Be prepared to engage with visitors and answer their questions:

Host or Hostess: You or your real estate agent should be present to greet visitors, offer tours, and discuss home features. Be friendly and informative without being overbearing.

Feedback Forms: Encourage feedback on the property by providing forms that visitors can fill out. This can provide valuable insights into what buyers like or dislike about the house.

6. Follow-Up: After the event, follow up with attendees who expressed interest:

Thank You Notes: Send a thank-you note to those who attended, expressing appreciation for their time and interest.

Follow-Up Calls: Make follow-up calls or emails to check if visitors have further questions or wish to discuss the property in more detail.

By meticulously planning and executing your open houses and private showings, you can increase the likelihood that attendees will have a positive experience, remember your property fondly, and move closer to making a purchase decision. This hands-on interaction often convinces a prospective buyer to make an offer.

Networking with Real Estate Agents: Leveraging Professional Networks to Reach Potential Buyers

While digital marketing and home staging play crucial roles in selling your home, networking with real estate agents can amplify your efforts by tapping into their professional networks and expertise. Real estate agents have connections and tools to expose your property to a broader audience of potential buyers. This section explores how to leverage these networks effectively.

1. Choosing the Right Agent Selecting an agent who is well-connected within the local market can be a game-changer:

Specialization: Look for agents who specialize in selling properties that have not sold in your area, as they will have relevant knowledge.

Local Expertise: Consider agents with a strong history selling homes similar to yours, whether luxury properties, condos, or family homes. They will likely have a large pool of potential buyers and know what sells well in your neighborhood.

Network Size: Ask about the size and scope of their professional network. This includes potential buyers and relationships with other real estate agents who can bring their clients to your door.

2. Agent-to-Agent Networking: Encourage your agent to leverage their network of fellow professionals:

Broker Open Houses: Unlike standard open houses aimed at potential buyers, broker open houses are specifically for local real estate agents who can recommend your home to their clients.

MLS Listings: Ensure your agent lists your property on the Multiple Listing Service (MLS), a primary tool agents use to find properties for their clients.

Real Estate Associations: Agents involved in real estate associations are typically well-connected, which can help you get your property noticed.

3. Utilizing Technology: Ask your agent about using technology to enhance exposure:

Virtual Tours: Agents can share virtual tours of your home in their newsletters, emails, or websites to engage local and out-of-town buyers.

Social Media and Email Campaigns: Experienced agents often use these tools to inform clients about new listings and market updates.

4. Networking Events: Participation in networking events can provide additional exposure:

Industry Conferences and Seminars: Agents who attend these

events can network with a wide range of professionals who might have clients interested in your listing.

5. Referral Strategies Discuss with your agent the possibility of a referral strategy:

Incentives for Referrals: Some agents offer incentives to other agents for referring buyers who close on a sale, which can motivate more agents to show your property.

Client Referrals: Encourage your agent to tap into their past client network for potential buyers looking for a new home.

6. Regular Communication: Maintain regular communication with your agent to keep your property top of mind:

Feedback and Updates: Regular updates from your agent about the feedback from showings and market changes can help you adjust your selling strategy as needed.

Marketing Adjustments: Discuss any necessary adjustments in marketing strategies based on the feedback received from the network.

Networking with real estate agents leverages their expertise, connections, and tools, significantly enhancing the visibility of your property. By collaborating closely with your agent and encouraging them to tap into their networks, you can reach a vast and diverse pool of potential buyers, increasing your chances of a successful sale.

Creative Selling Points: Identifying and promoting the unique features of your home.

Architectural Feartures: Look for unique architectural details that set your home apart, such as original hardwood floors, crown moldings, or an unusual layout.

Recent Upgrades: Highlight any recent upgrades you've made, such as energy-efficient appliances, smart home technology, or high-end materials.

Outdoor Features: Emphasize appealing outdoor spaces, whether it's an expansive backyard, professional landscaping, a swimming pool, or a well designed patio area

Historical Signifigance: If your home has historical signifigance or is located in a historically important area, make sure to promote this aspect.

Scenic Views: Does your home offer panoramic views or overlook water or cityscapes? Views can be a major selling point.

Unique Location or Benefits: Consider the location benefits that come with your home, like proximity to desirable schools, parks, public transport, or shopping districts.

CHAPTER 4: NEGOTIATION TACTICS

Understanding Buyer Psychology: Insights into What Buyers Are Looking for and How to Appeal to Their Needs

Effective negotiation in real estate isn't just about arriving at a favorable price—it's also deeply rooted in understanding the psychological factors that drive buyer decisions. This section explores the critical aspects of buyer psychology and provides insights into how to appeal to potential buyers' emotional and practical needs.

1. Recognizing Emotional Drivers: Purchasing a home is as much an emotional decision as a financial one. Buyers often make choices based on how a home feels, not just its price or features. Key emotional drivers include:

Security and Comfort: Buyers want to feel that the home will be safe and comfortable for them and their families.

Aspiration and Status: A home symbolizes personal achievement and social status for many.

Visual Appeal: First impressions are critical, as buyers often decide whether they can envision themselves in a home within moments.

2. The Role of Lifestyle Fit: Understanding the lifestyle a buyer is seeking can significantly influence how you market and negotiate the sale of your home:

Family Buyers: May prioritize safety, educational opportunities, and space for children to play.

Professional Couples: Might look for modern amenities, home offices, or proximity to transit and cultural hubs.

Retirees: Often value ease of maintenance, accessibility, and community activities.

3. Addressing Practical Concerns: While emotional factors are significant, practical considerations also play a critical role:

Value for Money: Buyers want to feel they are making a wise investment, so highlighting features that offer long-term value can sway decisions.

Flexibility and Potential: Showcasing a home's potential for customization or expansion can be appealing, especially to buyers who view properties as a canvas for creativity.

Maintenance and Upkeep: Emphasizing recent upgrades or low-maintenance features can alleviate concerns about potential ongoing costs.

4. Building Trust and Credibility: A successful negotiation relies on the buyer's trust in the seller and the transaction. To build this trust:

Transparency: Be open about the home's condition and any issues. Honesty helps build credibility and reduces the chances of negotiations breaking down at later stages.

Professionalism: Present all information neatly and professionally, from written descriptions to your interactions.

Responsiveness: Respond promptly to inquiries and be flexible in accommodating viewings, demonstrating respect for the buyer's interest and time.

5. Leveraging Fear of Missing Out (FOMO): FOMO can be a powerful psychological trigger in real estate negotiations, especially in competitive markets:

Highlight Demand: Subtly inform potential buyers of the interest other parties have shown in the home to create a sense of urgency.

Deadline Setting: Establish deadlines for offers, which can prompt buyers to make decisions more quickly and possibly bid higher to secure the home.

6. Understanding Negotiation Leverage: Be aware of the factors that give you leverage in a negotiation, such as:

Market Conditions: In a seller's market, you may be able to push for higher prices or stricter terms.

Home Condition: A home in excellent condition offers leverage because it's more appealing and less risky for buyers.

Your Flexibility: If you're not in a rush to sell, you have more leverage to wait for the right offer.

By understanding and addressing buyers' psychological needs, you can more effectively communicate the value of your home and negotiate terms that are agreeable to both parties. This approach facilitates a smoother transaction and helps you achieve a sale that meets or exceeds your expectations.

Negotiation Skills: Tips for Negotiating Prices and Terms Effectively

Effective negotiation is critical in securing the best possible price for your home and favorable terms to make the selling process smoother and more satisfying. This section offers practical tips for honing your negotiation skills, enabling you to confidently and tactfully navigate discussions with potential buyers.

1. Preparation is Key: Before entering any negotiation, ensure you are thoroughly prepared:

Know Your Bottom Line: Understand the minimum offer you are willing to accept and what terms are non-negotiable.

Market Knowledge: Arm yourself with current market data. Know how your home compares to similar properties in terms of price, condition, and location.

Anticipate Buyer Concerns: Be ready to address common concerns buyers may have about your property.

2. Maintain Flexibility: While it's important to know your limits, maintaining some flexibility can help close a deal:

Price Flexibility: If a buyer is close to your acceptable price range but not quite there, consider what terms might make a slightly lower price acceptable, such as a faster closing date or waived contingencies.

Terms Adjustment: Sometimes adjusting terms like closing costs or including certain appliances or furniture can be more cost-effective than altering the price.

3. Use Silence as a Strategy: Silence can be a powerful negotiation tool. After making an offer or counteroffer, give the buyer time to think and respond. This can prevent you from making unnecessary concessions out of a desire to fill the silence.

4. Communicate Clearly and Professionally: Effective communication is crucial.

Be Clear and Concise: Clearly articulate your points and reasons. Avoid overly complex explanations, which can lead to misunderstandings.

Stay Professional: Control your emotions. Treat negotiations as a business transaction.

5. Listen Actively: Listening is as important as speaking in negotiations.

Understand Buyer Motivations: Paying attention to what the buyer emphasizes can give insights into their priorities, which can be leveraged to create a more appealing offer.

Acknowledge Concerns: Show that you hear and understand the buyer's concerns, which can help build trust and smooth the negotiation.

6. Use Timing to Your Advantage: Timing can influence the dynamics of a negotiation:
Don't Rush to Lower the Price: Be patient if your home has just hit the market. Rushing to drop the price can signal desperation.

Time Your Concessions: Conceding at the right moment can turn the negotiation in your favor. For example, after the buyer has shown significant interest or made a concession.

7. Build Rapport: People prefer to do business with those they like and trust:

Find Common Ground: Small talk about shared interests can ease tensions and build a positive rapport.

Be Accommodating: Demonstrating a willingness to accommodate the buyer's requests within reason can make negotiations more amicable.

8. Document Everything: Ensure all agreed-upon terms are documented:

Written Offers and Counteroffers: Always have offers and counteroffers in writing to avoid any misunderstandings or disputes.

Final Agreement: Review the final sales agreement thoroughly to ensure all details are correct and reflect the negotiated terms.

By mastering these negotiation skills, you can engage in the process more effectively, making strategic decisions that lead to a successful sale. Remember, negotiation is not just about winning but about finding a mutually satisfactory conclusion to the sale of your home.

Dealing with Low Offers: How to Handle and Counter Lowball Offers

Receiving a lowball offer on your home can be disappointing and even frustrating, especially if you feel the offer doesn't reflect the actual value of your property. However, effectively handling such offers is a critical skill in real estate negotiations, as they can sometimes be turned into reasonable deals with the right approach. This section provides strategies for dealing with low offers constructively.

1. Stay Calm and Professional: The first step in dealing with a lowball offer is maintaining professionalism. Reacting emotionally can harm negotiations and potentially lose a buyer who might be persuaded to increase their offer.

Assess Buyer Intent: Try to understand the motive behind the offer. Some buyers start low as a negotiation tactic, while others might genuinely believe the home is overpriced. Sometimes, the offer might reflect their budget rather than their property valuation.

2. Evaluate the Offer: Before responding, take the time to evaluate the offer thoroughly in the context of current market conditions and your circumstances.

Consult Your Agent: Discuss with your real estate agent whether the offer is reasonable given market trends or if it's an outlier that should be countered more aggressively.

Consider Your Selling Timeline: If you are in a hurry to sell due to personal circumstances, you should be more flexible in your negotiations.

3. Respond Politely: Whether you choose to accept, reject, or counter the offer, respond politely. This keeps the door open for further negotiations.

Acknowledge the Offer: Thank the buyer for their offer and express appreciation for their interest in your property.

4. Make a Strategic Counteroffer: If you decide to counter, be strategic about how much to increase the counteroffer.

Justify Your Counter: When making a counteroffer, provide clear reasons why your home deserves a higher price, such as recent upgrades, unique features, or strong interest from other buyers.

Include Compromises: Show your willingness to negotiate by adjusting other terms, such as closing dates and contingencies, or even including certain home appliances or furnishings.

5. Highlight the Home's Value: Reinforce the value of your home by highlighting aspects that justify your asking price. This can include:

Unique Selling Points: Remind the buyer of any exceptional or highly desirable features of your home that increase its value.

Market Data: Present comparable sales in your area that support your valuation.

6. Set a Minimum Threshold: Decide in advance the lowest offer you are willing to accept. This helps avoid drawn-out negotiations that are unlikely to meet your minimum requirements.

Communicate Your Bottom Line: If repeated negotiations return below your minimum threshold, clearly communicate this limit to the buyer to set expectations.

7. Know When to Walk Away: Sometimes, the best move is to walk away from an offer that doesn't meet your needs, especially if the buyer isn't showing flexibility.

Non-Responsive Buyers: If the buyer isn't responding positively to counteroffers or providing justifications for their low offers, focusing on other potential buyers might be more productive. Effectively handling lowball offers involves patience, diplomacy, and strategic negotiation. By staying professional and open to dialogue, you can convert a low offer into a sale or move on to more promising prospects without burning bridges.

CHAPTER 5: LEGAL AND FINANCIAL CONSIDERATIONS

Understanding Contracts: A Breakdown of Common Legal Terms and Conditions in Home Selling

Navigating the complexities of real estate contracts is crucial to selling your home. These contracts are legally binding agreements and outline the rights and responsibilities of both the buyer and the seller. Understanding the common legal terms and conditions can help you avoid pitfalls and ensure a smooth transaction. This section provides a breakdown of key elements typically found in home-selling contracts.

1. Offer and Acceptance: The basic structure of any real estate contract involves an offer by one party and acceptance by the other. The buyer typically makes an offer, which the seller can accept, reject, or counter.

> Binding Agreement: Once both parties agree to the terms and sign the contract, it becomes legally binding.

2. Purchase Price: This is the amount the buyer agrees to pay for the property. The contract should clearly state the purchase price

and the terms of payment.

Earnest Money: A deposit made by the buyer to show their seriousness about the purchase, held in an escrow account until closing.

3. Contingencies: These are conditions that must be met for the contract to proceed. Common contingencies include:

Inspection Contingency: Allows the buyer to have the property inspected within a specified period.

Financing Contingency: Ensures the deal is contingent on the buyer obtaining financing from a lender.

Sale of Previous Home: Sometimes, the purchase depends on the buyer selling their current home.

4. Closing and Possession Dates: The contract should specify when the closing will occur and when the buyer will take possession of the home.

Closing Date: When the transaction is completed, the deed is transferred from the seller to the buyer.

Possession Date: When the buyer is entitled to take possession of the property. This can be the same as the closing date or specified as a different date.

5. Legal Descriptions: The contract should include a precise legal description of the property, not just the address. This description typically references lot numbers, block numbers, and subdivision names as recorded in county records.

6. Inclusions and Exclusions: Specifies which fixtures and personal property are included in the sale and which are excluded.

Inclusions: Items like appliances, light fixtures, or window coverings that will stay with the house.

Exclusions: Personal property that the seller will take with them.

7. Dispute Resolution: Specifies the process for handling disputes should they arise, including mediation, arbitration, or court action.

Mediation Clause: Requires that the parties attempt to resolve disputes through mediation before taking legal action.

8. Title and Warranties: Details about the title and any warranties being transferred with the property.

Clear Title: The seller must provide a title free of liens or claims.

Warranties: Any warranties that will be transferred to the new owner, such as a roof warranty.

9. Amendments and Addenda: Any changes or additions to the contract must be made in writing and signed by both parties.

Addendum: A document that modifies or adds to the terms of the existing contract.

Understanding these elements of your real estate contract will empower you to navigate the selling process more confidently and securely. Always consider consulting a real estate attorney to review the contract before signing to ensure that all terms are clear and your interests are protected.

Financial Planning: Managing Finances While Awaiting a Sale, Including Dealing with Ongoing Mortgage Payments

Selling a home can often take longer than anticipated, so homeowners must be prepared to manage their finances carefully during this period. Effective financial planning ensures you remain financially stable and meet ongoing obligations such as mortgage payments. This section provides strategies for managing your finances effectively while your home is on the market.

1. Budgeting for Extended Sale Periods: Start by revising your budget to accommodate the possibility of an extended sale period.

> Assess Your Cash Flow: Look at your income and expenses. Consider how long you can maintain your financial obligations if the sale takes longer than expected.
>
> Cut Non-Essential Spending: Temporarily reduce discretionary spending to preserve cash reserves.

2. Handling Mortgage Payments: Your most significant financial obligation is likely your mortgage. Here's how to manage it:

Communicate with Your Lender: If you anticipate difficulty meeting mortgage payments, contact your lender early. Lenders may offer forbearance agreements or temporary arrangements to reduce or pause payments.

Refinance Options: If the interest rates are favorable, consider refinancing your mortgage to lower your monthly payments. However, this option requires careful consideration, as it involves appraisal and closing costs.

3. Maintaining the Property: Even though funds might be tight, it's crucial to continue investing in essential home maintenance.

Prioritize Repairs: Address any critical repairs that could negatively impact the sale or lead to more significant issues later.

DIY Maintenance: Save money by doing some maintenance tasks yourself instead of hiring professionals.

4. Utilizing Savings and Emergency Funds: If you have savings or an emergency fund, decide how and when to use these resources.

Emergency Fund: Setting aside three to six months of living expenses is advisable in case of unexpected delays.

Investment Liquidation: Consider if it makes sense to liquidate other investments to cover living costs, being mindful of any potential tax implications or penalties.

5. Exploring Temporary Revenue Options: If the financial strain of waiting for a home sale is significant, look into temporary ways to generate income:

Rental Options: If you've already moved out, consider renting out the home or part of it as a short-term rental if local regulations allow.

Part-Time Work: Taking on part-time work or freelance projects can also supplement your income during this period.

6. Planning for Tax Implications: Be aware of potential tax implications related to your home sale and financial decisions during this period:

Capital Gains Tax: Understand how capital gains tax might

affect you if your home is sold. Specific tax rules regarding the sale of primary residences may benefit you.

Deductibility of Mortgage Interest: Mortgage interest payments and certain refinancing costs may still be tax-deductible.

7. Professional Advice: Consult with a financial advisor to review your financial strategies and a tax professional to understand the tax implications of your decisions:

Financial Advisor: Can provide personalized advice based on your overall financial situation.

Tax Professional: This will ensure that you make the most tax-efficient decisions regarding your property and income.

Managing finances during an extended home sale process requires careful planning and proactive management. You can navigate this challenging period without jeopardizing your financial stability by staying informed and prepared.

Tax Implications: Overview of Potential Tax Consequences of Selling a Home

Selling a home can have significant tax implications, and understanding these can help you plan more effectively and save money. This section outlines the key tax considerations associated with selling a home, including potential liabilities and opportunities for tax benefits.

1. Capital Gains Tax: One of the primary tax considerations when selling a home is the capital gains tax levied on the profit (gain) made from the sale.

Exclusion of Gain: If you have owned and used the home as your primary residence for at least two of the five years before the sale, you may be able to exclude up to $250,000 of gain from your income if filing as single or $500,000 jointly. This exclusion can be used multiple times over your lifetime but generally no more frequently than once every two years.

Calculating Gain: Your gain is calculated by subtracting the cost basis (generally the purchase price plus any improvements) from the selling price, less selling expenses like real estate commissions.

2. Reporting Requirements If you receive a Form 1099-S as part of the transaction, you must report the sale of your home on your tax return, even if you qualify for the exclusion and owe no tax.

Non-Qualifying Use: If part of the time you owned the home falls under "non-qualifying use" (not used as your main home, such as a rental or vacation home), you may owe tax on a portion of the gain.

3. Deductions and Adjusted Basis: Improvements and certain selling expenses can affect your home's cost basis, potentially reducing the amount of taxable gain.

Home Improvements: Adding the cost of home improvements to your home's basis can reduce the taxable gain. These improvements must add value to the home, prolong its life, or adapt it to new uses.

Selling Costs: Real estate commissions, legal fees, advertising, and certain closing costs can also be subtracted from the sale price to reduce the taxable gain.

4. Depreciation Recapture: For homeowners who have used part of their home for business purposes or rented it out, depreciation

taken during these periods is subject to recapture at a 25% rate.

Reporting Rental or Business Use: You must report depreciation recapture on your tax return for the years you claimed depreciation on the property.

5. State and Local Taxes: In addition to federal taxes, you may be liable for state and local taxes related to the sale of your home.

State Capital Gains Taxes: Some states also tax capital gains. The rates and rules vary by state, so consulting with a local tax advisor is essential.

Local Transfer Taxes: Some localities impose a transfer tax on the sale of property, which, depending on local law, can be the responsibility of the seller or the buyer.

6. Special Situations: Certain situations may affect the tax implications of selling a home.

Selling at a Loss: If you sell your primary residence at a loss, unfortunately, the loss is not deductible against other income.

Inheritance and Gifted Properties: Different rules apply for homes acquired through inheritance or as a gift, particularly in how the basis is calculated.

7. Consulting a Tax Professional: Given the complexities of real estate transactions and the significant impact of tax laws, consulting with a tax professional is advisable. They can provide guidance tailored to your situation, help you maximize your tax benefits, and ensure compliance with all relevant tax laws.

Understanding these tax implications can help you make informed decisions about the timing of your sale and how to handle your financial gains or obligations. Planning with the help of a tax professional can lead to substantial economic benefits and smoother transaction processing.

CHAPTER 6: WHEN TO CONSIDER ALTERNATIVES

Renting Out Your Home: Pros, Cons, and Considerations for Turning Your Property into a Rental

When your home isn't selling as quickly as anticipated, renting it out can be a viable alternative that offers financial benefits and other advantages. However, becoming a landlord comes with its own set of challenges and responsibilities. This section will explore the pros, cons, and critical considerations of turning your property into a rental.

Pros Of Renting Out Your Home

1. Steady Income Stream: Renting out your home can provide a consistent source of income that covers the mortgage and other property-related expenses.

2. Tax Deductions: Landlords can take advantage of tax deductions for rental properties, including depreciation, maintenance, repairs, property taxes, insurance, and management fees.

3. Property Value Appreciation: While your property generates rental income, it could also appreciate, potentially increasing your return on investment when you decide to sell.

4. Flexibility: Renting out your home provides financial flexibility while waiting for a more favorable real estate market to sell your property.

Cons Of Renting Out Your Home

1. Landlord Responsibilities: Being a landlord involves time, effort, and the cost of maintaining the property. You're responsible for repairs, tenant management, and complying with rental property regulations.

2. Potential for Problem Tenants: Dealing with tenants can sometimes be challenging. Potential issues include late payments, property damage, and legal disputes over evictions or deposits.

3. Market Fluctuations: Rental markets can fluctuate, affecting your ability to charge competitive rent and find tenants.

4. Capital Gains Tax Implications: If you rent out your property for more than three years, you may lose part of the capital gains tax exemption for primary residences when you eventually sell.

Considerations Before Renting Out Your Home

Understanding Market Rent: Research local rental markets to determine competitive pricing for your property. Tools like Zillow, Rentometer, or local real estate agents can provide insights into what you can realistically charge.

Legal and Regulatory Compliance: Familiarize yourself with landlord-tenant laws in your area, including rights, obligations, and any specific local regulations regarding rental properties.

Financial Viability: Calculate the potential rental income versus expenses like mortgage payments, property taxes, insurance, and anticipated maintenance. Ensure the numbers work in your favor.

Property Management: Decide if you will manage the property yourself or hire a company. Management companies can handle most landlord responsibilities but typically charge between 8% to 12% of the monthly rent.

Lease Agreements: Draft a comprehensive lease agreement that includes all necessary stipulations to protect your interests, such as security deposit terms, lease duration, pet policies, and maintenance responsibilities.

Preparation for Tenants: Your home may require modifications or upgrades to suit tenants, including safety updates, cosmetic improvements, and ensuring appliances are in working order.

Transitioning Back to Selling: Should you decide to sell your property in the future:

> Notify Tenants: Provide adequate notice to tenants as required by lease terms and local laws.
>
> Sale with Tenants: Selling a property with tenants can appeal to some buyers, especially investors. Alternatively, the property can be sold once the lease has expired.

Turning your unsold home into a rental can be beneficial if managed correctly. It requires a clear understanding of what it means to be a landlord and careful planning to ensure that it meets your financial goals and lifestyle needs.

Property Exchange: Exploring Less Common Options Like Property Swaps

When a traditional sale isn't progressing as hoped, homeowners might consider more unconventional avenues, such as property exchanges or swaps. This strategy can be particularly appealing in specific markets or under certain economic conditions. This section discusses the concept of property exchanges, their benefits, challenges, and key considerations.

What is a Property Exchange? A property exchange, often called a property swap, involves two property owners trading their properties. These exchanges can be direct swaps or part of a more complex arrangement involving multiple parties and properties.

Benefits Of Property Exchanges

Avoid Market Slowdowns: Finding someone willing to swap properties in a slow market can expedite the process without waiting for buyers.

Cost Efficiency: Swaps can reduce costs associated with selling and buying properties, such as agent commissions, closing costs, and market listing fees.

Tax Advantages: Property exchanges (especially those structured as 1031 exchanges in the United States) can offer tax deferral on capital gains under certain conditions.

Challenges Of Property Exchanges

Matching Property Values: One of the biggest challenges is finding a swap partner with a property that meets your needs and has a comparable value.

Complex Negotiations: Swaps can involve complex negotiations to ensure that both parties are satisfied with the terms, including the condition and valuation of each property.

Financing Difficulties: If mortgages are involved, both parties must secure new financing approvals or agree to take over each other's loans, which can complicate or hinder the process.

Considerations For Property Exchanges

Market Research: Thoroughly understand the markets of the properties involved. This understanding is crucial to ensuring a fair value exchange and anticipating market-related challenges.

Legal and Tax Advice: Consult with real estate attorneys and tax professionals. Property swaps involve intricate legal and tax implications that need expert guidance to navigate effectively.

Appraisals and Inspections: Both properties should undergo independent appraisals and inspections to confirm their market values and conditions, preventing disputes post-exchange.

Agreement Formalities: Draft a detailed agreement that outlines every aspect of the exchange, including timelines, responsibilities for expenses, and contingencies for unexpected issues.

Executing A Property Exchange

Finding a Swap Partner: Use online platforms dedicated to property swaps, network through real estate agents specializing in such deals, or explore local real estate investment groups.

Negotiation: Once a potential swap partner is found, begin

negotiations to align the terms of the exchange. This process is critical and can benefit from mediation by a real estate professional experienced in swaps.

Finalizing the Deal: After agreeing on terms and completing all necessary inspections and appraisals, close the transaction similarly to a standard property sale, ensuring all legal and financial documents are correctly executed.

Alternative Creative Solutions

Partial Swaps: If there's a discrepancy in property values, consider partial swaps where one party also pays a cash difference.

Temporary Swaps: For those not ready for a permanent swap, consider temporary swaps for a specified period, which can be an innovative solution for those needing a change or testing a new market.

Property exchanges represent a creative but complex alternative to traditional home selling and buying. While they are only suitable for some, they can provide a viable solution for homeowners stuck with a property that isn't selling conventionally. Proper guidance, thorough preparation, and a clear understanding of the process are essential to successfully navigating the intricacies of property swaps.

Temporary Solutions: Short-term Fixes While Waiting for a Buyer

When your home is lingering on the market without offers, consider temporary solutions to alleviate financial pressure or maintain the property's viability. These short-term strategies can provide relief while you seek a buyer, ensuring you remain financially and emotionally stable. This section explores several temporary fixes that can help homeowners manage the challenges of a stagnant listing.

1. Short-Term Rentals Renting out your property on a short-term basis can be a viable option, particularly in high-demand areas or during peak tourist seasons.

> Platforms like Airbnb: Use platforms like Airbnb or Vrbo to generate income. This approach can be especially beneficial if you live in an attractive area to tourists or business travelers.

> Flexibility: Short-term rentals allow you to keep the property available for showings to potential buyers.

2. Lease with Option to Buy Offering a lease with an option to buy can attract tenants interested in eventually purchasing but may need more time to be ready to commit.

> Attract Potential Buyers: This strategy can draw in those who need time to build savings for a down payment or improve their credit score.

> Income Stream: You'll secure a tenant and income while giving someone the chance to buy later, often at a predetermined price.

3. House Swapping for Vacations: If you're flexible with living arrangements, participating in house swapping can offset some of your living expenses.

> Vacation without Hotel Costs: This can be particularly appealing if you have another place to stay temporarily; you can enjoy a vacation without significant accommodation expenses.

> Maintain Property Care: Having people stay in your home can help maintain and deter potential security issues with an empty property.

4. Pop-Up Usage: If your home is located in a commercial area or suitable for events, consider renting it out as a pop-up space.

   Event Space: Rent your space for events, workshops, or galleries.

   Commercial Pop-Ups: Short-term leases to businesses for seasonal sales or promotional events can generate revenue.

5. Deferring Maintenance Costs: If you're tight on funds, prioritize essential maintenance while deferring less critical repairs.

   Essential Repairs Only: Focus on maintenance that preserves the home's integrity and safety but postpone cosmetic upgrades.
   Energy Efficiency: Small, cost-effective updates can reduce utility bills, such as sealing leaks or adding insulation.

6. Financial Assistance Programs: Investigate whether local government programs can assist homeowners struggling to sell.

   Tax Relief: Some localities offer temporary property tax relief for homeowners meeting specific criteria.

   Subsidized Loans or Grants: Check for programs that offer subsidized loans or grants to maintain properties during prolonged sales periods.

7. Revisiting the Market Strategy: While implementing these temporary solutions, it's crucial to reassess and adjust your market strategy regularly.

   Stay Informed: Keep up with local market trends and adjust your selling strategy accordingly.

   Feedback from Rentals: Use feedback from temporary tenants or event users to identify any issues with the property that might be affecting its saleability.

By employing these temporary solutions, you can mitigate some of the financial strain and maintain the appeal of your property while continuing to search for a buyer. These strategies help manage the home during uncertain times and potentially increase the property's exposure and desirability in the market.

CHAPTER 7: EMOTIONAL ASPECTS OF SELLING YOUR HOME

Coping with Stress: Strategies for Managing Stress and Maintaining Mental Health During the Selling Process

Selling a home can be one of the more stressful experiences in life, especially when the process extends over a long period. The uncertainty, financial pressures, and disruptions to daily life can take a toll on your mental health. This section provides strategies to help manage stress effectively during home selling, ensuring you remain resilient and emotionally balanced.

1. Maintain Regular Routines

   Daily Structure: Keep a regular daily routine as much as possible. Structured days with set times for activities like meals, exercise, and relaxation help maintain a sense of normalcy.

   Sleep Hygiene: Prioritize good sleep habits by maintaining consistent sleep and wake times. A well-rested mind is better equipped to handle stress.

2. Exercise and Physical Activity

Regular Exercise: Engage in regular physical activity. Exercise is a proven stress reliever and can improve your mood and decrease anxiety.

Outdoor Activities: Whenever possible, incorporate outdoor activities into your routine. Exposure to nature can boost your mood and reduce feelings of stress.

3. Stay Organized

Planning: Use planners, calendars, or digital apps to keep track of all tasks related to selling your home. Knowing what to expect each day can help reduce anxiety about the unknown.

Declutter: Keep your living space organized and clutter-free. A tidy environment can lead to a more peaceful mind.

4. Communicate Openly

Real Estate Agent: Maintain open lines of communication with your real estate agent to stay informed about the selling process. Regular updates can lessen feelings of uncertainty.

Support System: Discuss your feelings and frustrations with friends or family. Sharing your experiences can lighten your emotional load and provide different perspectives.

5. Mindfulness and Relaxation Techniques

Meditation: Practice meditation or deep-breathing exercises to manage acute stress and promote relaxation.

Mindfulness: Engage in mindfulness practices, which involve staying present and fully engaging with the current moment. This can help you avoid becoming overwhelmed by future uncertainties.

6. Set Realistic Expectations

Educate Yourself: Understand the current real estate market, including typical timelines and potential setbacks. Setting realistic expectations can help prevent disappointment and frustration.

Flexible Mindset: Be prepared to adapt your strategies based on market feedback. Flexibility can help mitigate stress when faced with delays or unexpected challenges.

7. Take Breaks When Needed

Mental Breaks: If the stress of constant showings or negotiations becomes too overwhelming, taking a short break is okay. Temporarily stepping back can help you regain your composure and perspective.

Leisure Time: Allocate time for enjoyable leisure activities. Whether reading, watching movies, or pursuing a hobby, taking time for yourself is crucial.

8. Professional Help

Counseling: If stress becomes unmanageable, consider seeking help from a mental health professional. Therapy can provide effective coping mechanisms to handle stress related to selling your home.

Managing stress during the home-selling process is crucial for your mental health and for making effective decisions about your property sale. By implementing these strategies, you can maintain your well-being and navigate the challenges of selling your home with greater ease and confidence.

Family and Relationships: Navigating the Impact of an Unsold Home on Family Dynamics and Relationships

The prolonged process of selling a home can strain your patience and your family dynamics and relationships. The uncertainty and disruptions associated with an unsold property might lead to stress and conflict within a household. Understanding and addressing these challenges can help maintain harmony and support among family members during this taxing period. This section explores how to navigate the impact of an unsold home on family dynamics and provides strategies for preserving and strengthening relationships.

1. Open Communication

   Regular Family Meetings: Hold meetings to discuss the selling process and family members' concerns. This keeps everyone informed and provides a platform for expressing feelings and concerns.

   Encourage Expression: Allow each family member to express their thoughts and feelings about the moving process. Children, especially, need to feel heard and reassured.

2. Managing Stress Collectively

Shared Activities: Engage in activities that the whole family enjoys. This can be anything from movie nights to outdoor activities, providing a needed break from home selling stress.

Support Systems: Lean on external support systems like friends and extended family. Having an outside perspective can help reduce tension within the home.

3. Maintaining Routines

Consistency for Children: Strive to keep children's routines as consistent as possible, including school activities, meal times, and bedtimes. Consistency in daily life can provide stability amidst the chaos of selling a home.

Shared Responsibilities: Distribute household responsibilities evenly to avoid resentment. When everyone contributes, it lessens the burden on any single family member.

4. Addressing Financial Stress

Transparent Budgeting: Be transparent about financial issues with appropriate family members, particularly with partners or spouses. Discussing financial plans and constraints can reduce misunderstandings and stress.

Plan for Contingencies: Have a clear plan for managing finances if the property takes longer to sell than expected. Knowing there is a plan in place can reduce anxiety for everyone.

5. Consider Family Members' Needs

Individual Needs: Pay attention to each family member's specific needs. For example, if a family member is studying or working from home, ensure they have a quiet space during house showings or open houses.

Emotional Support: Recognize signs of stress in each other and offer support. Sometimes, simply acknowledging the situation's difficulty can be very comforting.

6. Seeking External Help

Family Counseling: If tensions rise significantly, consider seeking help from a counselor specializing in family dynamics. They can provide tools and strategies to improve communication and resolve conflicts.

Relocation Services: If the move is imminent, engaging services that help families relocate can ease the transition and reduce the logistical stress on everyone involved.

7. Keeping the End Goal in Mind

Discuss the Benefits: Regularly remind family members of the sale's positive aspects, such as moving to a better location, upgrading to a bigger home, or being closer to extended family.

Visualization: Help your family visualize the positive outcome of selling the home. Whether decorating a new bedroom or exploring a new neighborhood, focusing on the future can be motivating.

Navigating the emotional terrain of selling a home requires empathy, patience, and proactive communication. By implementing these strategies, you can help mitigate the impact of an unsold home on your family's dynamics and relationships, ensuring that the journey, while challenging, is navigated with mutual support and understanding.

Moving Forward: Staying Positive and Proactive When Sales Plans Stall

The journey of selling a home can sometimes feel like a waiting game with an unpredictable end. When sales plans stall, maintaining a positive and proactive attitude is essential for your well-being and the eventual success of your home sale. This section provides strategies to stay motivated and forward-looking during these potentially challenging times.

1. Adjust Your Perspective

    Focus on What You Can Control: Concentrate on aspects of the sale you can influence, such as improving home staging, enhancing curb appeal, or revising your marketing strategy.

    Long-Term Vision: Remember why you decided to sell your home. Whether relocating for a job, downsizing or providing a better lifestyle for your family, remember the long-term benefits of persevering.

2. Set Small, Achievable Goals

    Incremental Objectives: Break down the sales process into smaller, manageable tasks. This might include weekly goals for decluttering, making minor repairs, or following up with your real estate agent.

    Celebrate Small Wins: Recognize and celebrate when you achieve these smaller goals. This can help build momentum and maintain a positive outlook.

3. Stay Organized

    Maintain a Schedule: Keep a detailed schedule of daily tasks and goals. Staying organized can reduce feelings of chaos and help you manage your time more effectively.

    Regular Reviews: Review your selling strategy with your real estate agent to ensure it aligns with current market conditions.

4. Keep Learning

Educate Yourself: Stay informed about the real estate market by reading articles, attending webinars, or speaking with professionals. Understanding market trends can help you make informed decisions and adjust your expectations.

Feedback Loop: Use feedback from potential buyers to make adjustments. Constructive criticism can be invaluable, whether about the home's appearance, price, or marketing approach.

5. Engage in Self-Care

Physical Activity: Regular physical exercise can significantly reduce stress and improve mood.

Hobbies and Interests: Engage in activities unrelated to the home-selling process. This can divert your mind from the stresses of selling and recharge your emotional batteries.

6. Connect with Others

Support Networks: Lean on friends, family, or support groups who understand what you're going through. They can offer encouragement, advice, and a sympathetic ear.

Professional Help: If you find it particularly difficult to stay positive, consider speaking with a counselor or therapist who can provide skilled support.

7. Plan for the Next Steps

Preparation for Future Moves: Start planning your move, even if the sale date still needs to be finalized. Research potential new neighborhoods, schools, and other relevant interests. This preparation can help you feel proactive and ready for the change.

Financial Contingency Plans: Develop a financial backup plan if the sale continues to be delayed. This might involve reassessing your budget, exploring temporary income options, or refinancing your current mortgage to reduce monthly costs.

8. Maintain Flexibility

Open to Change: Be open to adjusting your plans based on the sale's progress. Flexibility can reduce stress and make you more adept at handling unexpected challenges.

By staying positive and proactive, you can navigate the stagnation in your sales plans more effectively. Keeping your end goals in mind, celebrating small successes, and maintaining your mental and physical health are all crucial strategies that empower you to keep moving forward, regardless of the pace of the sale.

CONCLUSION

Navigating the Challenges of an Unsold Home: A Summary of Key Points

As we conclude "Stuck in Place: Navigating the Challenges of an Unsold Home," we must reflect on our journey together, exploring the myriad strategies and insights designed to help you move forward with selling your home. From understanding why homes don't sell to discovering practical steps to enhance your home's appeal and facilitate a sale, this book has covered extensive ground.

Here, we summarize the key points and strategies discussed, ensuring you have a concise guide to refer back to as you navigate your home selling process.

1. Understanding Why Homes Don't Sell

Overpricing: Recognizing the dangers of setting an unrealistic price and learning how to determine a competitive yet fair market price.

Condition of the Property: Emphasize the importance of your home's condition and aesthetics and the need to make necessary repairs and updates to attract buyers.

Marketing Missteps: The critical role of effective marketing, including professional photography and utilizing digital platforms to reach potential buyers.

Market Dynamics: Understanding how local and national market conditions affect home sales and how to adapt your strategy accordingly.

2. Preparing Your Home for Sale

Home Staging: Implementing staging techniques to make your home more appealing during showings.
Essential Repairs and Improvements: Prioritizing repairs and improvements that increase your home's value and appeal to buyers.

Professional Photography: Leveraging high-quality images to effectively showcase your home's best features.
Creating a Welcoming Atmosphere: Ensuring that each showing leaves a positive impression on potential buyers.

3. Innovative Marketing Strategies

Digital Marketing: Maximizing social media and online real estate platforms to enhance visibility and attract buyers.

Open Houses and Private Showings: Organize effective events, allowing buyers to experience your home firsthand.

Networking with Real Estate Agents: Utilizing the networks of professionals to expand your reach.

Creative Selling Points: Highlighting unique features and benefits of your home to stand out in the market.

4. Negotiation Tactics

Understanding Buyer Psychology: Gaining insights into what

drives buyers and how to appeal to their needs and desires.

Negotiation Skills: Mastering the art of negotiation to achieve the best possible outcome regarding price and terms.

Dealing with Low Offers: Strategies for handling and countering offers that exceed expectations.

5. Legal and Financial Considerations

Understanding Contracts: A breakdown of common legal terms and conditions in home selling.
Financial Planning: Managing finances effectively while awaiting a sale, including dealing with ongoing mortgage payments.

Tax Implications: Navigating the potential tax consequences of selling a home.

6. When to Consider Alternatives

Renting Out Your Home: Weighing the pros and cons of renting your property.

Property Exchange: Exploring less common options like property swaps.

Temporary Solutions: Implementing short-term fixes while waiting for a buyer.

7. Emotional Aspects of Selling Your Home

Coping with Stress: Strategies for managing stress and maintaining mental health during selling.

Family and Relationships: Navigating the impact of an unsold home on family dynamics and relationships.

Moving Forward: Staying positive and proactive when sales plans stall.

Understanding and implementing the strategies discussed in this book can enhance your ability to sell your home effectively, even in challenging conditions. Remember, every home selling journey is unique, and maintaining flexibility, patience, and a proactive attitude is crucial in navigating this complex process successfully.

APPENDICES

The appendices provide detailed explanations of real estate terms, and a resource guide to support sellers through the home selling process. This supplementary material is designed to enhance your understanding and management of the sale of your home.

Appendix A: Glossary of Terms

Capital Gains Tax: Tax on the profit from selling property or an investment.

Contingencies: Conditions that must be met for a real estate contract to be fulfilled.

Curb Appeal: A property's exterior attractiveness as viewed from the street.

Earnest Money: A deposit made by the buyer to demonstrate their serious interest in the property.

Equity: The value of the homeowner's interest in their home, calculated as the home's value minus the mortgage balance.

FSBO (For Sale By Owner): A method of selling property without the aid of a real estate agent.

Lien: A legal claim or hold on a property as security for a debt or charge.

MLS (Multiple Listing Service): A database established by real estate brokers to provide data about properties for sale.

Staging: Decorating a property to make it more appealing to potential buyers.

Appendix B: Resource Guide

Websites

Realtor.com: Offers comprehensive real estate listings and resources for sellers and buyers.

Zillow.com: Provides home value estimates and other helpful tools in home selling.

Trulia.com: Features detailed neighborhood information, including crime stats, school ratings, and community reviews.

Books:

The Honest Real Estate Agent by Mario Jannatpour: Guides new agents and sellers through the real estate process with integrity.

Selling Your House: Nolo's Essential Guide by Ilona Bray: Offers practical advice from preparing your home for the market to closing the sale.

Professionals:

Local Real Estate Agents: Contact local real estate offices for agents with expertise in selling homes in your area.

Certified Residential Specialist (CRS): CRS is the highest credential awarded to residential sales agents, managers and brokers. CRS agents have verified experience and a record of successful transactions.
Search for a CRS in your area at: https://find.crs.com

Home Stagers: Consult the Real Estate Staging Association website to find certified professionals in your region.

Financial Advisors and Tax Professionals: Look for certified professionals via the Financial Planning Association (FPA) and the American Institute of CPAs (AICPA).

ABOUT THE AUTHOR

Morgan C. Sloan

Meet Morgan C. Sloan, one of Florida's premier real estate brokers. His passion for real estate began when he was a boy in Tampa. As a child, his fascination with properties was as clear as Florida's blue skies, and this enthusiasm led him down a path of dedication and professionalism that shines brightly in his work today. His motto? 'Turning dreams into addresses.'

This early passion for real estate continued to ignite Morgan's path as he transitioned to Orlando. His 20+ years and over 300 transactions as a broker and investor have been an unwavering testament to his devotion to this industry.